FACING IT FORWARD

FACING IT FORWARD

Ordinary Women of the Bible with
Extraordinary Assignments

by Nicole Jackson

Text Copyright © 2019 Nicole Jackson

All Rights Reserved

Dedication

This book is dedicated to women who are in a season of uncertainty and desire to understand their purpose. Women who are going through, but are willing to trust God, so they can move forward. You do not have to go through life's circumstances alone. God is with you. May we all learn how to trust God, face our circumstances and move forward.

To my daughters Alexandria White, Cierrah Ffrench and Ashelynn Jackson, granddaughters Naomi White and Camdyn Ffrench, I am so blessed to have you as my biggest blessings. May the Lord use you greatly as you journey through life seeking opportunities to give God glory. To my sisters, Brandie, Adrian, Ginette, Sara, Renita, Veronica, and Melanie, thanks for your love and always lending me your ears. To two very special women in my life Debra Sims, and Keitha Norman. Thank you for providing for me.

To the women of the Myers, Bush, Jackson and Goshe Family. We are strong women who know Jesus Christ is our everything. We praise Him for choosing us for His purposes in our prospective places. He has blessed us over and over again and has delivered us out of dangers seen and unseen. May this book be held as a record to the young ladies of our family, of how God uses ordinary women for extraordinary assignments. No one has to know our name, but we have a responsibility for others to know our God. I love you and dedicate this book to you.

Acknowledgements

As I a look back over my life, I am reminded of how special I am to God. I never realized the magnitude of His love until He gave me the assignment of researching women in the Bible He used mightily. He wanted me to know He created me for His purpose and there was no situation or person that could change His love and plans for me. This was good news. The search began and I was amazed at the women in the Bible I had never been introduced to. I read their stories and realized they were just like me. I was led to study several books of the Bible, where I could see God at work in the lives of His daughters. I was so encouraged and excited to discover such a diverse group of women, I couldn't keep their stories to myself. What was I to do with these new revelations? The Lord allowed me to set up a women's Bible Study conference call, entitled "Saturday Breakfast", to discuss these ordinary women of the Bible, with women who desired to know God's purposes for their lives. These women were hungry for the Word and committed to the weekly call. We learned so much. I am so grateful that God allowed us to talk about other women in a Godly manner. Thank you, ladies of the "Saturday Breakfast" Bible Study for allowing me to teach, learn and pray with you. Did I say cry as well?

I am thankful for: my husband Antonio, who cares for me, travels with me and is elated about the assignment God has given us. A man of God who proves each day that God and family are always first. To my Mothers In love, Helen Chappell and Step mom Pricilla Goshe, thanks for praying for me and believing in the gifts that God has given me. To Babbie Mason, my book-writing coach, you saw something in me that I didn't see in myself and you took the time to work with me and push me to share my gifts with the world. I am forever grateful to God for you as a coach, publisher and friend. To my Editor and Book Designer, Dr Julie A. Cross, thank you for your awesome work. To my Women's Bible Study Group, Gloria Daniels, Elaine Reid, Teresa

Harris, Mary Hollis, Felicia Leslie, Topeka Robinson, Tracy Hamilton and Yolanda Smith, thank you for keeping me in your prayers and studying the Word of God with me. To Minister Vicki Tucker, my best friend, sister and biggest cheerleader. Thanks for always being there for all that God has in store for whatever assignment is on my life. To Evangelist Mary Williams, God used you to plant the seed. Thank you for your continued prayers and words of wisdom. To Lakecia Gunter, thank you for being a friend and allowing God to use you as a template for what women endure in the workplace. To my sister prayer circle, Elder Michelle Williams, Elder Debra Gulley, Minister Regina Randle, Apostle Mary Richardson, Pastor Marilynn Woods-Lee, Minister Rebecca Richardson-Autry, Lady Debra Wesley-Bell, Minister Newlene Dean, Minister Brigida Fisher, Minister Michelle Holiday, Minister Mattie Broxton, Stephanie Artis, Evangelist L. Taylor and Chaplain Karen Ellis-Wilkins. Your prayers are appreciated. To my sisters of "Where Are My Sisters", who selflessly serve women of our communities. Terri Marshall, Nicole Dixon-May and Minister Brigida Fisher. To the women of St. John Divine M.B.C. of Milton, FL, thank you for your love and support. To the Milton, FL and Haines City, FL communities. Thanks for your support. Blessings to my Whataburger Family, the most awesome Brand in the QSR Industry.

To you the wonderful readers of this book, I pray this book awakens you to the endless possibilities God has in store for you. I hope you will be motivated to be the best "you", that you can be. You have a purpose and God will use you right where you are. I pray you see God's hand moving through the stories of the women in this book and realize whatever you are facing, you are not alone. In the midst of your storms, you are still purposed for greatness. Just trust God and face your circumstances as you continue to move forward. Don't look back my sisters. God still uses ordinary women for extraordinary assignments. Keep moving toward your destiny.

Most of all, Lord I praise You for entrusting me with this assignment. You know the thoughts You think toward me. They are good and not of evil to give me an expected end. You have anointed me to teach, testify and take Your Word to the nations. I am forever grateful to be an instrument used for Your glory.

Table of Contents

Dedication — 5

Acknowledgements — 7

Foreword — 15

Introduction — 17

Dauntless Daughters of Zelophehad — 21

Chapter One Questions — 30

Judicious Jael — 33

Chapter Two Questions — 42

Wise Woman of Thebez — 45

Chapter Three Questions — 52

Witty Woman of Abel — 55

Chapter Four Questions — 62

Jehosheba and Athaliah — 65

Chapter Five Questions   *71*

Ambitious Achsah   75
Chapter Six Questions   *82*

Dorcas the Disciple   85
Chapter Seven Questions   *92*

Conclusion   95
Action Plan   *99*

About Nicole   *101*

Foreword

Nicole and I grew up in a small town in Florida called Haines City. We've known each other since 5th grade. Our lives revolved around faith, family, and community. Our families stressed the importance of a good education, service to the community, and a firm foundation in the word of God. We live in a world where the yellow brick road has many paths and can take us on so many incredible journeys. After high school, I went to college to pursue degrees in computer and electrical engineering and after graduating I went to work in corporate America. I quickly became an executive in a Fortune 100 company and had the pleasure of traveling all over the world. By society's standards, I had made it and was living the American dream. However, I wanted more. I began to ponder what my true purpose and calling in life was supposed to be. I began to desperately seek the Lord's face and study His Word to understand what He had "purposed" me to do in the world. I knew being an engineer was what I was doing, but I knew he called me to do more. What I love about Nicole and her book is that she realizes that we all want to know why we are here and what we are "called" to do. If we are to know what we are called to do, we must have a relationship with the One who "called" us, Jesus Christ. Each of us will go through a discovery process just like the women she unveils to us in her book. Nicole chooses to illuminate eight distinct stories of ordinary women like you and me. Each of the women in these stories were designed for greatness, designed for His purpose before they were conceived—Just like you! As you read this book, I believe it will ignite a fire inside you, a desire to live life on purpose, on assignment and on mission for the One who created you to make a difference in this world.

Lakecia Gunter

Vice President, Intel Corporation

Introduction

Has there ever been a time in your life when you've questioned your value? Are you mentally and emotionally drained from trying to figure out what direction your life should be going in? Do you find yourself asking these questions?

"What is my purpose in life?"

"Will I ever walk into my destiny?"

"Can God use an ordinary woman like me?"

And the one that plays on repeat like songs on your iTunes playlist,

"What is It that I'm missing?"

Now press **STOP**.

I'll pause while you take a moment to wipe that single tear that's streaming down your face as you read this.

My sister, you are not alone. Every woman has a situation that we will refer to as our "IT". My "IT" may not be the same as yours, but "IT" must be dealt with. An "IT" is a circumstance or situation that makes you doubt that God has a plan for your life. That thing that keeps you up at night wondering if you will ever breathe normally again. It's a devastating storm that seems to last longer than normal. What is "IT" for you?

I know at times it seems like life has come to a stand-still. It can look as if everyone around you is prospering while your vision remains just a dream. But I encourage you to hold on and "let patience have her perfect work, that ye may be perfect and entire wanting nothing". (James 1:4) Patience will work for you, if you let her!

Make no mistake. What you are facing is hard, heart-wrenching and heavy, but do not tuck your tail and run! Facing "IT" with a determination to move forward, is the only way to move through the preparation needed to overcome and live out your purpose. You are being prepared for your destiny and what you are going through will mature you and make you stronger. Don't dodge "IT". This is your preparation before elevation.

Prepare for the Lord to take you on a journey that will shift your perspectives. Wrong perspectives limit your ability to experience where the Lord is taking you. Where is He taking you, you might ask? He is taking you through "IT" to your divine destination. Just keep the faith.

Remember God is the Author and Finisher of your faith. He has prepared a path before you that only you can travel.

Allow the Lord to use this book to strengthen your faith and help you navigate through the challenging events in your life by giving you examples of ordinary women of the Bible with extraordinary assignments. Women you don't hear about on Women's Days or at Women's Conferences. This book represents stories of ordinary women, like you and me, facing "IT" forward, representing God's presence, power and purpose. Each may have a different struggle and result, but they were made for the very thing God used them to accomplish.

As you look at their struggles and observe their obedience, you will find you have more in common with these women than you think. Let this be your last day of toiling with "IT". God has extraordinary plans for you.

A Prayer for my Friend

Heavenly Father,

I thank You for choosing your daughter for this assignment.

I ask that You lead and guide her into her destiny

Strengthen her when she gets weak

Comfort her when she feels alone

Use her to strengthen others.

Remove all distractions from within and around her

May she face it forward and see what You have purposed for her future.

Amen

1

Dauntless Daughters of Zelophehad

Be careful for nothing; but in every thing by prayer and supplication with thanksgiving let your requests be made known unto God. Philippians 4:6

The Request

I am still waiting! Waiting for that big moment to happen in my life, that will show me that I was destined for greatness after all. I've been counting my days for a while. When will it be my turn? Why can't I ever seem to catch a break? Then "this" happened and has sent me over the edge. Why me?

Are these your thoughts from day to day? Are you weighed down, worn out and willing to throw in the towel? "This is IT!" you exclaim. What is it that you have allowed to steal your focus? Is it a loss of a job or loss of a loved one? What tragic event has happened in your life that has caused you to write yourself out of God's plan?

Do you know nothing can stop what God has purposed for you? There is nothing bigger than God. Not even your circumstances. God knows and cares about the things that cause us pain. He will walk you through even this.

In tough times your thoughts may be scattered, but Deuteronomy 31:6 says, "Be strong and of good courage, fear not, nor be afraid of them." The trials of life may take your focus for a time and stir up your emotions, but allow the Lord to teach you how to face it! You're allowed to cry. But keep pursuing what God has purposed for you. He is with you and will never leave you nor forsake you. Whatever you are facing, face it forward and continue to follow God's plan. Your best days are ahead of you, even when trials and tribulations seem to dictate differently. Remember you are never the only one who has had to face challenging circumstances.

In the Bible there are five sisters that will help you see that you are not alone and there is purpose and praise located in your pain.

These five sisters in the Bible give us an example of facing unforeseen circumstances while moving forward. Their story is located in the Old Testament Book of Numbers 27. I would love to talk about them as individuals, but this would break up the purpose in which God has announced them together. They are called "The Five Daughters of Zelophehad." They are sisters who experienced a tragedy that would change their lives forever.

Unforeseen Circumstances

I know the feeling of experiencing a tragedy all too well. When my mom died from cancer, I was devastated. It was the hardest thing for me to accept. She was only 46 and I was 8 months pregnant with the granddaughter she would never meet. I felt as if someone hung up the phone on me while I

1. Dauntless Daughters of Zelophehad

was speaking mid-sentence, leaving me with just the sound of a dial tone humming in the background. I wanted to scream, "Hold on mom, don't hang up. I have so much more to say"! But it was too late. My heart was broken. Pat, Brandie and I had to realize we lost more than our mother. Our time had ended as her son and daughters. August 1, 2000 was a day we would never forget.

If that wasn't enough, while preparing for her funeral, my brother received news that the mortgage company would be foreclosing on our childhood home. Our childhood home was in foreclosure and my mother never uttered a word. Not only were we planning her funeral, we were preparing to remove our family pictures from the walls.

We were in shock! How would my grandmother receive this news? With only a 6th grade education, my grandmother worked hard and paid off this home, taking out a second mortgage to help mom pay for her wedding costs. This house represented my grandmother's blood, sweat and tears. There were great memories, meetings and I guess too great of a mortgage for my mom to handle while sick. How could we push forward in the midst of this tragedy?

Pushing Past the Pain

These Five Daughters of Zelophehad are the epitome of pushing forward in a time of tragedy. These five sisters faced a future that would result in a greater loss than the mortgage of a home. They were facing the loss of their inheritance.

Mahlah, Noa, Hoglah, Milcah, and Tirzah experienced the loss of a parent. Their father died. This is something no one wants to go through. As your heart goes out to them, try to imagine the pain of this family, especially when the Bible never speaks of their mother and they had no brothers. They were the only ones left in their family. All they had was each other.

The Five Daughters of Zelophehad grew up during a time when women didn't have rights. The male figure was the spokesperson for the family and the only one who was eligible to keep land and carry on the family name. This family had no sons and no male heirs. They were bound by culture, customs, and the laws of their time. The law of inheritance stated, "If a man had no sons, his inheritance would be transferred to the next of kin, males only". With no male figure to speak for them, their future looked grim. Who would help them keep their inheritance? This law had never been challenged, so it would be best for them to drop their heads, walk away and mourn the passing of their father.

Have you ever forgotten how God made a way out of no way? Have you given up and stopped moving forward? What gives you strength is remembering your testimonies of God working miracles in your life. Remembering God knows the plans He has for you. Plans of good and not of evil, to give you an expected end. You must expect God to take your circumstances and work it out for your good.

God would take this planned event in the lives of these sisters and use it for His purpose. I know you're wondering what good could possibly come out of this tragedy?

As you reflect over your life, have you found that your worst moments are now your best testimonies? When it seems like you wanted to quit and retreat, a glimmer of light made its way through and changed your view of your situation. How does this happen? We know this is all God's doing. He loves you so much and orchestrates these events to allow you an opportunity to trust Him and build a relationship with Him for future assignments.

1. Dauntless Daughters of Zelophehad

The same God who walked my family through our tragedy, walks with you and walked these five sisters into the opening of what seemed to be a closed case. He was setting these ordinary women up for an extraordinary assignment. God's daughters deserve an inheritance too. Would they face their circumstance or settle with the law of their times?

These sisters had a choice to make. Either they could stay in a state of mourning about their father's death and lose their inheritance or they could challenge these laws of discrimination and stand up for their rights to keep their father's property, so his name would live on. Which would you do? Let's see how God worked this situation out.

The Preparation

They made a choice to stand up for their rights and their father's name. No time to sleep in. Too much was at stake. It was time to prepare their case. It's time for you to prepare as well. When preparing to stand for what's right, it's not wise to charge into the court room without conducting your research and having your facts in order. You must anticipate what the prosecutor may ask, secure your evidence and trust that God has it already worked out in your favor. Have you done your homework?

These daughters were ready. They didn't allow their emotions to ruin their future. Their research and facts were in order and now it was time to travel to the appointed destination to present their case. They moved forward. The Bible tells us the daughters traveled to the place where Moses, God's leader and intercessor for His people and Eleazer, the priest were taking a census. They were to count the males of each tribe for when the time would come to divide the land that God promised them as an inheritance. Did you catch that? These daughters were in route, at the right time, to the very backdrop they needed to present their case. It was time to be counted and you are about to see God's plan unravel before your very eyes. Look for the favor of God in all things.

Get out your popcorn and tissues. You're about to go on an emotional roller coaster. These women, who should have been home cleaning and cooking, were walking up to the country club for men challenging the membership. I feel empowered already. They did not roll their necks, wave their hands or make a scene, but they were surely seen by all who were in attendance.

This scene reminds me of the 1979 American drama film called Norma Rae, starring Sally Fields. An ordinary single mother, making minimum-wage as a cotton mill worker, who challenged the mills poor work conditions, which killed her father, forcing her to challenge the company by organizing a union and protesting. We as women have a voice even when we are told to be silent. God hears our prayers and is moved when His daughters cry out to Him.

The Presentation

Can you hear the music playing in the background letting us know that something big is getting ready to happen? "Order in the court." I can hear the judge say, "Are you ready to make your opening statement?" "Yes, your honor, we are." They start with a little history to set the scene. They tell Moses about their father, addressed possible gossip about him and go right in with their main question.

They asked this question, "Why should the name of our father be done away with among his family because he hath no son?" Then they shared what they desired. "Give unto us therefore a possession among the brethren of our father," the daughters said to Moses. How bold and courageous was that?

1. Dauntless Daughters of Zelophehad

They didn't say can we have a possession, they said "give us." They believed they had a right to secure an inheritance. This stirred Moses to seek God, because He couldn't give them something he didn't have. This was not his decision. The land belonged to God. Now Moses must go to the Owner of the land of promise to present their case.

Who have you spoken to about your problems? Did you go to the right person who can take your concerns directly to the Owner? We have Someone who intercedes for us. He is our Advocate and a spiritual attorney who speaks for us without ceasing and His name is Jesus Christ. He is our Lord and Savior. We can cast our cares upon Him because He cares for us.

I can imagine Moses' concern for them. He was an awesome man of God. He had a family. A sister by the name of Miriam and a brother, Aaron. His carrying their care before God showed his character. Can you see God routing His daughters to Himself?

These ladies wanted an answer. This was unfair to daughters and widows alike. They stood to challenge a system that would affect their future.

A Posture of Waiting

It is now a waiting game. Like the daughters of Zelophehad, you must be patient and await the timing of God. You must also approach the throne of God boldly, yet humbly. He is holy and righteous and you are to reverence Him. Philippians 4:6 tells us "Be anxious for nothing; but in everything by prayer and supplication with thanksgiving let your requests be made known to God." In order for them to receive an answer, they first had to make a request. Until Moses came back with the verdict, they continued to wait.

These sisters didn't waste time crying about their situation to others. They didn't run around the camp looking for someone to attend their pity party. The took "It" to the Intercessor.

The Settlement

God spoke to Moses as He called the sisters by name. How did God know their names? How does God know your name? God is omniscient which means He is all-knowing. The Creator knows His creation. God had written their plans and now they were walking in their assignment.

Read Numbers 27:1. "God said to Moses, the daughters of Zelophehad speak right: thou shalt surely give them a possession of an inheritance among their father's brethren; and thou shalt cause the inheritance of their father to pass unto them." Let's press rewind. God said they spoke right when they learned that they didn't have the right to speak. God drew His daughters to Him for care. He knew their situation and became their only solution. He is a father to the fatherless, making them eligible for an inheritance.

Their blessing was on the way and would remove worry, weight and change things for women forever. Why? Because they trusted God and faced their "it" forward. Their obedience would not only bless them, but all women of their time. That's right! Break out your tissues. Every woman from that day forward stood to receive this same blessing as these daughters did. Women who never lifted a finger toward the cause, and women who didn't even know what was taking place, would hear the Good News and benefit from the boldness of these sisters. This was a change that would remain forever. No woman would ever suffer through the loss of an inheritance again. This includes you, your children and your children's children. It was an all-inclusive command from God. Never again would His daughters be removed from His will.

1. Dauntless Daughters of Zelophehad

Think on These Things

What qualified the five daughters of Zelophehad to be used by God? What was special or unique about them? God qualifies and this was His purpose for them.

These daughters were living testimonies that women who are voiceless can still come out victorious if you follow God's plans. No one can orchestrate an amazing outcome like this, but God. Had they known the canvas used for this beautiful picture would be painted on the background of their father's death, would they have volunteered for this assignment? Like many of us the answer would be no. This would definitely be a class you would drop from your schedule.

What a class. This tragedy was unforeseen, but the training that took place was well worth it for those involved. This is a celebration for all. In death, the very life of all women was restored. These ordinary women of God's Word have taught us how to get up from where we are located and move towards the results we are looking for. Let's just say thank you to God's first paralegals. What a presentation!

Five Daughters of Zelophehad — They Waited for IT!

Chapter One Questions

Dauntless Daughters of Zelophehad

1. What tragedy have you experienced? Has it clouded your vision?

2. How have you experienced God's love during unforeseen circumstances?

3. Do you listen for God's voice when everything around you screams, "Just give up"?

4. What Scriptures are your "go to", when your mind needs renewal?

1. DAUNTLESS DAUGHTERS OF ZELOPHEHAD

A Prayer for My Sister

Lord, I thank You for trials and tribulations that have curved my sister's perception of Your love and comfort. Your strength is made perfect in weakness and I pray she recognizes that You are in control of every aspect of her life, even when she does not understand. Teach her how to push through until her breakthrough. May my sister learn how to continue on the journey and receive everything You have in store for her. In the Name of Jesus, Amen.

2

Judicious Jael

Blessed among women shall Jael the wife of Heber the Kenite be, blessed she shall be above women in the tent. Judges 5:24

When Opposition Becomes an Opportunity

This ordinary housewife picked up a hammer, a tent peg and killed a man. Just like that! I know this sounds like an episode of the television show "How to Get Away with Murder", but the star in this story wasn't Viola Davis. This was not a Netflix series. This was a real story located in Judges chapter 4 of the Bible. This story is about a woman whose life literally changed overnight. She was suddenly faced with great opposition because she had a life or death choice to make. A choice that would leave the best of us shaking our heads saying, "I would never do that in a million years."

Have you experienced moments in your life, when strange things happened and you whisper to yourself, "No one will ever believe this!" If not, then hold on tight because this is one of those moments that will leave you speechless.

Woman of God, you are probably wondering, what could you possibly learn from this woman? She doesn't fit the description of the kind of woman we think God would use. If the truth were to be told, none of us would qualify either, based on our own merit.

Thank God for His unmerited favor called grace. We are imperfect human beings striving to serve our perfect God. Remember you are a work in progress. Everything isn't always what it seems. There is much to glean from this ordinary woman of God. This woman was specifically chosen for you. Pay attention to your opinions about her to see if you are limiting what God can do in your life.

The Occupation

This ordinary woman is none other than a woman by the name of Jael. She was the wife of a blacksmith from the Kenite tribe. A tribe that never had a permanent place to call home. They pitched their tents in rural places and would pack up and move as their animals needed pasture. Jael had the responsibility of pitching tents, as did all women of her day. She repetitively performed these duties each time they would settle in their new location. You can assume she was seasoned with using hammers and tent pegs. What strength she must have. Can you also imagine the frustration of packing up so often? You never get an opportunity to settle down in one place for any length of time.

Jael's was an ordinary housewife. Being a housewife wasn't unusual, given the times she lived in. Women didn't have career choices like you and I do today. Women were restricted to taking care of the family, completing household chores and were most often unappreciated for the work they did. This ordinary housewife had a job she couldn't quit.

2. Judicious Jael

About 10 years ago, I had an opportunity to be a stay at home mom. I was always a hard worker and sometimes held down two jobs. A time came in my life when I was tired of the hustle and bustle of punching a time clock. It was time for me to be at home and take care of my family. I had often dreamed of staying home and imagined how fascinating this would be. Oh, the plans I made. Plans to prepare extravagant meals for my family, help my children with their homework and spoil my husband.

Can you shout "Good intentions!"? I found out quickly, it was not what I envisioned it to be. It was like I was subject to everyone, but never the topic of anything. Decision were being made for me. I had even become my children's Uber driver. So, I said "Bye, bye" to being at home for that season. I love my family, but this just didn't work for me.

What about you? With all of the love, care and effort you put forth, are you appreciated by your family? Being a housewife introduced me to the hard labor and un-appreciation that comes with the duties performed. I have a great appreciation for the many women who have mastered taking care of their families with such pride, but as for me, back to work I went.

Relationship Issues

Jael's tribe during their wanderings, found themselves drawn to the children of Israel. Israel befriended them. But things changed over time. Israel was influenced by their environment and disobeyed God. They compromised all that God instructed them to do by entering into Canaanite paganism. They knew better and served other gods. This saddened God and angered Him. They had to pay for their disobedience against God's instructions. As do you and I.

God punished them by sending them into the hand of their enemy and a military commander by the name of Sisera. He was cruel and ruled over the children of Israel in their captivity for twenty years. When Israel was in bondage what was the Kenite tribe doing? Were they helping their friends? No. They left them high and dry? So much for friendship.

Jael and her husband pitched their tent in the middle of the land. They were in between the children and the enemy of Israel. She was caught in the middle.

Her Pain

What was Jael thinking and who cared? God cared even when it seemed no one else did. In her life being a woman with no voice, she could speak to God through her heart. How did she feel about her tribe leaving their friends in their greatest time of need? Awful I'm sure. Jael had a heart for the children of Israel because she was able to hear about Israel's God.

The Bible tells us in Romans 10:17, "Faith comes by hearing and hearing by the Word of God."

Jael believed in Israel's God. But she would have to honor her husband's choice to leave them in their suffering. How could she prove she wasn't against God? There was no open door for her to walk through. She was faced with going along to get along. For the time being she would have to be the good housewife and stay quiet. The liberty to think for one's self and make good choices are sometimes taken for granted. Can you put yourself in Jael's shoes?

After 20 years of being in bondage, the Bible tells us the children of Israel cried out to the Lord. They prayed desperately for help. God heard them and

2. Judicious Jael

had His plan in place for their rescue. God raised up leaders to take out the enemy, so the children could be freed.

These next words are a game changer. God spoke through a prophetess by the name of Deborah these words in Judges 4:9. "Certainly I will go with you," said Deborah. "But because of the course you are taking," as she spoke with Barak the military leader God chose, (who was lacking in trust) "the honor will not be yours, for the LORD will deliver Sisera into the hands of a woman." So Deborah went with Barak to Kedesh.

Did you catch it? Before this battle would be fought, God had already planned for a woman to be involved and she would be successful. How do you know? Because God said the honor would be given to a woman. This woman had a purpose and she hadn't been introduced to it yet. Now pause and meditate on this thought.

When Opposition Shows Up

Have you ever been minding your own business and suddenly you find yourself in the middle of drama? Well pay attention because Jael will soon be faced with a choice to make.

The battle had begun. Barak and his army were winning against Jabin's army. They killed every member of the army, but Sisera got away. Sisera ran on foot and landed at the door of the tent of his old friend Heber's wife, Jael.

Jael knew that Israel was in a battle for their freedom. How could she help? How could she show Israel that just because her husband moved her away, doesn't mean she desired to be separated from her friends and God?

When Opportunity Knocks

What will you do when Sisera, the enemy shows up to your door? Will you retreat or face this situation? Remember, he's a dirty fighter. Sisera was not invited, neither was he expected. Now think about it. As unpredictable as this may seem, can you see how God is working this out? Jael is now faced with a choice. God has given her an opportunity to choose whose side she was on and her opportunity suddenly showed up at her doorstep.

Wisdom at Work

Jael invited Sisera inside her tent. This was wisdom at its best. The enemy was on her turf. She was wise enough to conclude that if anyone saw her outside her tent with Sisera, they would assume she was against Israel and kill her. Also, she knew by Sisera showing up to her tent, he would kill her in time as well. This ordinary, voiceless woman would have to think fast, as her life depended on the choices she would make.

Did Sisera have good intentions? No. A rule of hospitality in those times was no man could enter another man's tent when he was not home. Notice Sisera never asked for her husband and he desired to enter her tent in her husband's absence. Jael knew his actions showed his intentions. This was not good. She knew his plot, even when she didn't understand God's plan.

She told Sisera "Fear not." (These words were what she needed most!) She needed him comfortable with her, as she was filtering through her next move. He laid down and she covered him with a blanket. Next, he asked her for a drink because he was thirsty. She used wisdom again. Instead of giving him water to rehydrate him and give him energy, she gave him milk to put him fast asleep. Who knows what he would have done to her, if he regained his strength?

2. Judicious Jael

He had one last request before he closed his eyes to sleep. This thing he asked, confirmed and exposed him for the enemy he was. He asked her to stand at the door of her tent and if anyone asked if he was there, to tell them no. Checkmate! He asked her to lie. This was not a good situation for Jael. She must make a move and she'd better move fast.

She Hit the Nail on the Head

As Sisera fell asleep, Jael took what she had at hand to take care of the problem she had in her tent. What could she do against one of the most ruthless men alive? He was stronger than her and more skilled in battle.

She used what she did every day, as she was most familiar with its ins and outs. Everything she needed was at her fingertips. Jael picked up her hammer and tent peg and with all of her strength, she hammered the tent peg through the temple of Sisera, fastening him to the ground. Right there in her tent, he died. Jael killed Israel's enemy.

The Perfect Witness

God immediately sent a witness to what she did and Israel entered into peace for 40 years. Her offering was accepted because peace showed up. What Jael accomplished not only blessed her, but it blessed the entire land. This hidden figure conquered the enemy by trusting God and using what she held in her hand each and every day. It seemed as if she didn't have choices, but her life set her up for the opportunity. Her choice set her up for eternal life and He is doing the same for you.

Now having all of the details, is your opinion of her the same as it was in the beginning?

This teaches us that things aren't always as they seem. In the beginning of this story, it seems as if this was 1st degree premeditated murder. She seemed to be a woman that should be doing life in prison. But God interceded and saved her. During the times she thought no one cared, God heard her heart and shared that He had an extraordinary assignment planned for her all along. In the same way, He has an extraordinary assignment planned for you.

Her husband's ties to the enemy did not condemn her. The Bible tells us in Romans 8:1, "There is therefore now no condemnation to them which are in Christ Jesus, who walk not after the flesh, but of the Spirit." God gave her an opportunity to choose for herself.

Think on These Things

God had everything under control. We thank God for routing Jael's opportunity to her front door. As the saying goes, "When opportunity knocks, open the door," and she did just that.

God has everything planned to work in your favor as well. Deborah and Barak wrote a song about these events as they praised God. And yes, the woman that would receive the honor for this victory was Jael.

Be open to God's purpose for your life. It's not a one size fits all. Never say what you wouldn't do. You never know how God will orchestrate your break-through. Let's face it, this was unbelievable and hard to wrap our heads around, but God wants us ready at a moment's notice to be used by Him in any situation. Men and women alike. And by the way, never say I wouldn't do that in a million years." You may have to eat your words.

2. Judicious Jael

Jael represents strength, wisdom and every one's right to choose. You are never allowed to play the middle. Choose this day whom you will serve.

Judicious Jael — She Nailed IT!

Chapter Two Questions

Judicious Jael

1. In what area of your life are you the most complacent?

2. Do you go along to get along because of your perception of your worth? If you do, why?

3. Name three of your greatest strengths.

4. How might God use your strenths to advance His kingdom?

5. How do you push through your times of weakness?

2. JUDICIOUS JAEL

A Prayer for My Sister

Father, thank You for giving my sister an opportunity to use what You have given her for the betterment of others. Teach her to use wisdom when making the choices You have given her. Help her to discern when You are directing her, especially when it seems she has nowhere to turn. In Jesus' name, Amen.

3

Wise Woman of Thebez

I can do all things through Christ who strengthens me. Philippians 4:13

Determined

There was a time in my life that I felt there was nothing special about me. Sometimes I even felt no one would miss me if I disappeared. I tried to reinvent myself to become someone everyone could accept, yet it never prospered me anything. I became numb to the good that was happening in my life, while embracing my failures. Like Charlie Brown's best friend, Linus Van Pelt from the comic strip, Peanuts, who clung to his security blanket, my low self-esteem traveled with me everywhere I went. I wondered if I would ever be successful. My mundane life consisted of the same old routine activities every day. I am a fast-food trainer. Who cares? Yet God has made me visible.

How do you see yourself? Do you only see failure? Sometimes no matter how much you try to finish strong, it seems like you could have done better.

For example, I have a few friends, (like myself) who struggle with weight loss. We have a number in sight, but struggle when it comes to celebrating milestones. Does this describe you? Each step seems like it's not enough. No matter the achievement, it's treated like a negative. If it's ten pounds, you may say you wanted to lose fifteen.

Are you treating the blessings of God like this? When God blesses you, is it hard to celebrate because you don't feel deserving? You may need training on how to recognize, receive and rejoice in the blessings of God.

The Bible says, "Rejoice always, I say"! How often? Always! Are you thankful for everything the Lord has done for you? Recognize God's movement, even in the small things because if you don't, you could miss Him working in your life.

On the Grind

There is an ordinary woman in the Book of Judges 9, who's name wasn't mentioned, but her story was told. She stands as an example of what your everyday, repetitious activities can become in the hands of God.

She was a woman in days of old, who worked hard in the field. Her job was grinding wheat. This was her responsibility day in and day out. This was considered woman's work. Can you imagine the muscles in her arms? What a workout. But doing this everyday can become redundant. Can you imagine your inner struggle, if you only ground wheat every day? Where is the glory in this? This is like working in a fast food restaurant every day or working at the daycare center. This task seemed meaningless because she was always on the grind.

3. Wise Woman of Thebez

Remember everything isn't always as it seems. The very thing you may consider less, God considers it more. I call these "mustard seed moments." These moments are necessary to show God can do much with little.

This woman was living in a town called Thebez. A town that suddenly became under attack by a blood thirsty, power seeking, enemy approaching her city to overtake it by burning it down. This enemy was proven. He burned a neighboring city and killed thousands. Lives were at stake and fear had overtaken the city.

What's in Your Hands?

What do you do when "life happens" and you are overtaken with fear? You use your weapons to combat the enemy. You will find out specifically the weapons that work in situations like these.

The Bible says, God didn't give us the Spirit of fear, but of power and of love and of a sound mind. 2 Tim 1:7. At least we know fear is a spirit that doesn't come from God, so fear has got to go!

This woman and her city didn't invite this attack. It just showed up.

Have you ever been minding your business and going about your day and suddenly something comes from nowhere and presents itself in a way that rattles your bones? Those situations that leave you speechless and running for your life?

Sometimes when you feel life is meaningless and routine and you're not thankful for the little things, God allows something to come your way to awaken you to the greatness that is within you. He sets up a lab class to show you in practical ways, what He has placed on the inside of you. That thing on the way is bigger than your skills, bigger than your status, bigger than your finances, but never bigger than your God. He needs you to know that you are fearfully and wonderfully made and you are created to overcome. He also gives you time to practice and become familiar with your tools.

This uninvited predator came her way, and her response was to flee from where she was. Her first instinct was to run. Are you a runner? Do you run from your problems? You're not alone. Many have run away from the unfamiliar.

It's not the running that God is concerned with. It's Who you run to in your time of trouble. Psalm 50:15 says, "Call on me in your time of trouble and I will deliver thee."

When trouble finds you, who do you call on? This woman and the people of the city ran away from the enemy, into the strong tower of the city. It looked as if she didn't face her fears. Looks can be deceiving. She was routed to the only place of protection.

She arrived at her appointed destination, the strong tower of Thebez. She was climbing the stairs of the tower, trying to make her way to the top. I wonder how far she had to run to reach her destination?

Sometimes you don't know your own endurance until the enemy pushes you into your destiny. How far and how high will you go in the Lord for your situation to be fixed?

When the enemy arrived, there was nowhere else she could go. She couldn't outrun what was chasing her down. She had to face the enemy. But she wouldn't be facing him alone.

3. Wise Woman of Thebez

He began to start the fire that would bring her down. You know like the lies your so-called friends speak about you. He was firing her up. But he didn't realize her position in the Tower. She was up and he was down. She was inside the strong tower and he was trying to come up. She was behind a door that he didn't have the power to open. Sounds like the perfect condition to win a battle that was never hers in the first place.

When you run to the Strong Tower (Jesus Christ) and trust His protection, you are at a vantage point the enemy will never reach. His intention was to destroy her and the citizens of the city, but God had a different plan. Did the enemy have her cornered or did God create an opportunity to use her against the schemes and tactics of the enemy? I'm going with the latter. How about you? What are you thinking?

Do you really think our faithful and intentional God, would forsake His daughter? You have to believe Him at His Word. He will never leave us nor forsake us. That is a promise. He is the way out of no way.

Who will show up and rescue her? Truly there is a man who would step up and save the town. Nope not for this assignment. There was only One who was orchestrating the city's rescue. It was God working everything for their good.

It's in Your Hands

What instrument would He use to take the enemy out? God can use that thing that you considered meaningless. He uses that thing that you think has no value. That blessing that you won't celebrate. The thing you lay down to pick up something else you think is better. What is it that is big enough or heavy enough to take out one who has experience killing, stealing and destroying God's people?

Facing IT Forward

God uses you! He sent His Son, Jesus Christ to die and He defeated death and the grave. The Spirit of the Lord raised Him from the grave and He is seated at the right hand of the throne in Heaven. The same power is on the inside of you.

The answer is within you!

Jesus defeated our enemy for us. So how can God teach you that you have nothing to be afraid of? He does this by teaching you how to stand suited with the whole armor of God, against the wiles of the enemy. God teaches us how to contend for the faith.

This ordinary woman seemed to be no match for the enemy. But the enemy didn't recognize what she had in her hand.

As the enemy tried to push his way through the door of the tower, God used His daughter to pick up the upper millstone - you know that millstone that is used to grind wheat into grain. That was the very thing that was familiar to her. It was an instrument that she handled day in and day out. She was empowered to pick up the stone that she was familiar with, like David when He fought Goliath. She picked it up and released it and God did the rest.

She dropped the millstone from an elevated place and as it was traveling down, God guided it and the weight of it crushed the enemy's head. Yes! God used a woman for this assignment. Just like the assignments He has planned for you. A rock - the Solid Rock, once again took the enemy out.

Her daily grind was practice before the stand-off. Your ordinary is an extraordinary secret weapon that the enemy doesn't expect. Don't despise the day of small beginnings.

3. Wise Woman of Thebez

God knows what He wants to use in your life. Celebrate what He is doing, step by step. Who you are and what you do is meaningful. Everything He causes your hands to touch is a blessing. You must practice saying, "God can use even this for His glory!"

Think on These Things

The power of the Lord on the inside of you can save a life, a family or even a city if you will just release the stone. Releasing it sends the enemy fleeing.

The Bible says, the enemy, Abimelech, asked his servant to take his sword and kill him, so it wouldn't be said that he was killed by a woman. That's how important you are. The enemy doesn't want it said that he was defeated by a daughter of the King. Even after his servant struck him with the sword, the news spread that the wise woman of Thebez killed the enemy and saved the city. She faced it forward and others were blessed by her actions.

The enemy can't change your story. He can't rewrite what God has written. This unnamed woman was raised up for a time such as this and so are you. Take your position without taking what He is doing presently for granted. Get on your grind! It will soon pay off.

Wise Woman of Thebez — She Dropped IT!

FACING IT FORWARD

Chapter Three Questions

Wise Woman of Thebez

1. Are you appreciative of the job God has given you?

2. Who do you run to when trouble comes?

3. Name a person you consider a hero. What did they accomplish and how have they influenced you?

4. How can you cause the heavy weighted situations in your life to work out in your favor?

3. Wise Woman of Thebez

5. Is it easy for you to let go of things that weigh you down or do you tend to hold on to them?

A Prayer for My Sister

Father, Thank You for being our Strong Tower – the place we can run into for safety and refuge. I need You to prepare my sister for opposition. Teach her how to run to You in all things. You will never leave her, nor forsake her. Yes! You are her Strong Tower. Teach her how to seek high ground and let go of things that weigh her down. Strengthen her when things get heated. Help her to understand that You have given her the power through Your Word, to quench every fiery dart that comes her way. In the name of Jesus, Amen.

4

Witty Woman of Abel

But the wisdom that is from above is first pure, then peaceable gentle and easy to be entreated, full of mercy and good fruits, without partiality and without hypocrisy.
James 3:17

Wisdom Wins

Care for Community

    Growing up, I was always astounded by my grandmother's wisdom and her love for our community. She was a woman of faith, respected and known for her home remedies. People in our community would come by and sit with her for hours intrigued at how much knowledge she had in the area of health and wellness. Even though she only had a 6th grade education, you would have thought she had a PHD from some fancy medical school. I remember when I was twelve years old and sick with a cold. She made me this concoction that she would heat on the stove. It contained lemon, ginger and a few other items I dare not mention. It tasted absolutely awful, yet after drinking it, my cold was soon gone. She has now gone on to be with the Lord and I miss her so much. She was nurturing and her concern for others flowed throughout our family and community. My grandmother is my inspiration. Even though she didn't have much, she always used what she had.

You my friend, like my grandmother have something special to give to the world as well. By nature of you reading this book, I am going to assume you are a woman who's willing to use what you have, to be a blessing to others. But who inspires you? Is it a family member, friend or maybe someone you've read about?

Who Inspires You?

If you are lacking inspiration, let me invite you to a place where I meet up with ordinary women, who had extraordinary assignments on their life. These are the type of women you want in your circle. Our meeting place is no secret clubhouse for girls. It's in a public place called the Bible. There are so many inspirational women in the Bible and I specifically would like to introduce you to a woman who has blessed me in times when I felt I didn't have much to offer. Have you ever had days like this?

This woman makes her appearance in the Holy Scriptures in the book of 2 Samuel 20:14-22. The Bible doesn't give us her name or her family history, but it does gives us her location. She lived in a city north of Israel called Abel-Beth-Maachah. A city that became popular after becoming a battleground between two allies, as if it were the Bible day version of the TV show "Cops." Her city was on the brink of destruction and innocent lives were at stake. This woman was concerned for her city. What could she do to save it? She did what I hope you are inspired to do in times like these.

4. Witty Woman of Abel

She took on the city's problems as her own. She faced a situation for others so her community could have peace. She used what God gave her to make a difference. Not a gun, knife or a group of ladies with picket signs in their hands. She used her voice.

This woman left the comfort of her home, risking her life, to face Joab, the commander of King David's army about what he was doing to her city. What does that say about her concern for others? Did I mention this is during a time when women didn't have a voice and were defined by their husbands? What a backdrop! Can you imagine the thoughts that were going through her head? Was she afraid? Did she want to quit? The Bible doesn't say, but she stood in the midst of adversity for her city. This assignment was bigger than her.

Character is Important

2 Timothy 1:7 tells us, "For God hath not given us the spirit of fear, but of power, and of love and of a sound mind." This is the perfect scripture to declare when fear tries to enter your mind.

She fearlessly cried out in front of the wall this army was battering for the commander Joab to come hear what she had to say. She desired to speak directly to the person in charge. How courageous was that! But she showed humility when she asked him for permission to speak. She couldn't afford a misstep, for much was at stake. She also referred to herself as a handmaid, showing respect for his position. These character traits she is displaying, gives us a pattern to model. But aren't you curious to find out what she would say to convince this man to spare her city? There has to be a mighty speech or a special recipe, like the concoction my grandmother made, to cure the cold this city was going through. Things were getting heated.

She proceeded to give him a taste of her city's history, which revealed her to be a woman of wisdom and knowledge. Only one who was actively involved in her community could share its roots. Now for her request. She told him she was faithful as a citizen of Israel and she desired peace. I'm sure he felt her passion. Can you feel her passion coming through these pages? But this next thing she did was brilliant. Are you on the edge of your seat yet? Notice the shift. She mentions he would be destroying the very inheritance that God gave Israel. Truly this commander wouldn't desire to destroy what God gave the children of Israel, as he was of the chosen himself. This woman who should have been seen and not heard, made Joab remember the God he served. That was her secret recipe. Two tablespoons of using what you have, mixed with a teaspoon of courage, compassion and a conversation about God, saves communities.

She knew she had his attention when he replied he did not desire to destroy the city. He stated his case and asked her to deliver the troublemaker Sheba, who hid in her city and he would leave the city peacefully. Wait a minute! Is this military commander really negotiating with an old woman with no credentials?

This is a Romans 8:31 moment when the Bible says, "What shall we say to these things? If God be for us, who can be against us?" What an unusual outcome. She needs to run for governor.

This wise woman of Abel agreed to his terms and told him the enemy's head would be thrown over a wall to finalize their deal. She then gathered the people of her community and through her influence, caused them to actively participate in saving their city.

4. Witty Woman of Abel

The people of Abel were successful in finding Sheba. They cut off his head and threw it over the wall as promised. The enemy was no more. Joab blew the trumpet and the city was left unharmed.

It's Over

You might ask, how could an old woman speak a few words that changed the heart of a great commander and influence a whole city to move on one accord? The answer. It was by the anointing that God placed on her life. He gave her an opportunity to use her gift. She faced it forward. But would you look at your life through that same lens? There is an appointed time for your gift to come forth.

The Journey

What did you glean from her life? Did she inspire you to leave your comfort zone and get involved in your community? Glad you paid her a visit. She had much wisdom to share.

As we journey down her path, I can't help but think about how many excuses she could have given God to remain comfortable. She could have stated she was too old or she was a woman. She could have said it wasn't her problem, but she focused on God's will for the future of others, no matter the cost. It was her sacrificial love for God and His people that God used to save the city.

John 3:16 says, "For God so loved the world that He gave His only begotten Son, that whosoever believeth in him should not perish but have everlasting life." It is in the giving of ourselves that we find fulfillment. God modeled the behavior He desires to see from you.

FACING IT FORWARD

Think on These Things

Are you ready now to move from where you are to face your destiny? Everything you need is within you. You may not have what my grandmother had. You may not possess the same character traits of the witty and wise woman of Abel, but you are anointed to do great things for the Kingdom of God. You have wisdom, insight and an understanding of the situation you are facing. You are unique. You have traits that God has placed on the inside of you. Remember, no one can beat you at being you." What's your first step?

Will you start a neighborhood watch, check in on the elderly or babysit someone's child? You can begin right where you are. You decide, but remember you are not alone. Everything is a process.

First, expect an awesome ending to your story. Next, trust that God will bring opportunities before you to allow you to use the gifts, talents and abilities He gave you.

Lastly, embrace the gift that God has given you. Remember it took pressure to expose her purpose and the same God, who chose the Witty Woman of Abel, has chosen you to accomplish much. Wisdom always wins.

Witty Woman of Abel — She Spoke IT!

Chapter Four Questions

Witty Woman of Abel

1. Are you actively involved in your community? Why or why not?

2. Are there women in your community that you admire for their service? For what reasons do you admire them?

3. What are some of the contributions you have made in your community?

4. Why is it important to have a good reputation and model Christ-like behavior?

4. Witty Woman of Abel

5. When you speak, are people moved to listen and jump into action?

A Prayer for My Sister

Father, I thank You for surrounding my sister with good neighbors. I pray she is grateful for the opportunity to love and serve the needs of her community. Keep her focused on what's going on around her and help her to model Jesus Christ everywhere she goes. Make her aware when things are against Your will and use her as Your representative when wisdom is needed to settle disputes. In the name of Jesus, Amen.

5

JEHOSHEBA AND ATHALIAH

For God has not given us the spirit of fear, but of power, and of love and of a sound mind. 2 Timothy 1:7

Beauty and the Beast

Family is everything! Having a family that's perfect, loves you and supports you through the good and bad is what's known as a "dream family." Would you like to be a part of this family? Who wouldn't? Now, wake up, because a "dream family" is just that, a dream! You may have found out already that there is no such thing as a perfect family here on earth. We all need God's grace and mercy to learn how to love, laugh, and live in harmony with one another.

The Bible tells us, "All sin and come short of the glory of God." The key word is "All."

Families make mistakes and sometimes even hurt you. Even though it may not be intentional, there are many pain-points that damage relationships. To put it plainly, families have "fall outs." There are families that fight during funerals, family reunions and even when they are just fellowshipping together. Sometimes it's hard to recover from the fall outs and this causes separation. How do you recover from that? What are some things your family is disagreeing about right now?

If you believe your family may need to lie down on Dr. Phil's couch for a few therapeutic sessions in order to tell their story, let me introduce you to a family that was truly evil and terrorized many.

The Family

Remember this name Jehosheba. A woman of the Old Testament book of 2 Kings Chapter 11, who grew up with an evil stepmother in a family that killed God's people and prophets with no remorse. They were not followers of God. They were self-seeking and served idol gods. Jehosheba's grandfather was none other than King Ahab, who was the King of Israel. He was an evil man who was killed during a battle when his plot back-fired. Jehosheba's grandmother was Jezebel, who was more evil than her husband, Ahab. She met her demise when she was thrust out of a window, trampled by horses and eaten by dogs. The only thing left of her were her palms, feet and skull (I know, right?) Through several generations, this family personifies wickedness. What kind of family was this? Yes, I was thinking it too. "My family is not this bad on our worst day!"

Jehosheba's stepmother (Ahab and Jezebel's daughter) Athaliah was just as evil. There is a saying that the "chip from the old block doesn't fly far." This is true more than you know. Athaliah was mean, power hungry and bitter. Her husband and son were killed in battle and the city of Judah was without a leader. There were many successors, but Athaliah being true to her family's evil influence, killed every heir to the throne, (So she thought) so she could

5. Jehosheba and Athaliah

rule. She was drunk with power and the people would suffer under her leadership.

Who in your family, influences other members in a negative way? Hopefully no one. Most grandmothers I know love and care for their grandchildren. But, this woman killed her grandchildren. She didn't care who she had to sacrifice to get what she wanted. That's not family or the will of God.

The Bible tells us "Thou shall not kill." Yet, this woman killed without a second thought. It's mind-boggling. Women are considered nurturers, yet she shed innocent blood. Who would you kill, to move up? Athaliah was a product of what she was exposed to.

It is very important that we build our family up and leave long-lasting legacies that glorify God. Athaliah pursued the things of this world outside of God's will. She positioned herself instead of serving the only wise God who had a plan for her life. For six years she reigned over Judah as the people were oppressed by her and it looked as if she had everything she wanted. Did you know that everything is but for a season? Looks can be deceiving.

Self-Appointed Power

Ecclesiastes 3:1 says, "For everything there is a season, and a time to every purpose under the heaven." She thought she out-smarted God when she appointed herself as the ruler of Judah. Do you know someone who backstabbed others to get the position they are in today? Remember, only when we do the right things, with the right motives, will things turn out right. Blinded by greed, she thought her plan worked, but God's plan was happening right under her nose. She was so caught up in herself she didn't notice, her fearless step-daughter Jehosheba was in the palace during this time of the massacre of her grandchildren and was able by the strength of God, to sneak one of the youngest of their heirs, (her nephew Joash) and his nurse out of the palace. She hid him in the temple, where she and her husband, the high priest Jehoida, served. Yes, Jehosheba was the wife of One who feared God and was used to save an heir to continue the family line that our Savior, Jesus would travel through. God used a woman. Are we getting the thread that is going through this book? There is yet another woman who faced it forward, that God used to save the family line of Jesus. A secret spy, in the right place at the right moment, focused on Kingdom work.

Right when the devil thinks he has won, God uses what man least expects. He uses you! Jehosheba escaped unnoticed and she and her husband, High Priest Jehoida, taught him the way of the Lord for 6 years. She placed her life on the line to preserve the Davidic line. What courage this ordinary woman had. What she did was selfless and scary I'm sure. But she persevered because of her faith in God.

Can God use you in tough situations, so the life and legacy of your family can be preserved? Can you rise above the gossip, your family's reputation, your opinions and mostly your emotions, to be used by God for that great thing that will change everyone's life forever?

Jehosheba was a member of a bad family yet believed in a great God. She didn't allow her family's history or the actions of others to influence her. She didn't use family as an excuse. She went through a brutal, trying time and experienced the death of her nephews. She couldn't save them all, but she was able to be used to save one.

Sometimes you may believe that the task before you is too great. You may not understand how to win because your opponent appears to be on top. I tell you my friend, the devil is a defeated foe and makes fake appearances seem believable, but it's a smoke screen. You have already won. Obedience and trust are the keys to walking out right in front of the enemy. God never fails. The devil cannot stop what God has started. What God has purposed for you to accomplish, makes you unstoppable.

Why would God show you a picture of a corrupt family and then share the triumph of a member of the same family? I believe God wants you to know that you have a choice to break the cycle in your family and choose God over the enemy. He is giving you hope. You are not doomed or trapped. God always finds a way. He will even use you to achieve it if you are willing.

Jehosheba took a risk to save a member of her family during a time when women were not considered fearless or strong. She was an ordinary woman of God with an extraordinary assignment. A chosen vessel. Do you see how God will use the unassuming, the under served and even the under dog for His purpose?

The Paranoia

Her stepmother Athaliah heard there was an heir that survived her killing spree and was livid. She ran through the streets of Judah screaming treason. She felt betrayed. Now how could a murderer scream treason? How did this heir get past her? It was time for her to pay. Everyone who disobeys, God will repay. Romans 12:19 says, "Dearly beloved, avenge not yourselves, but rather give place unto wrath: for it is written, vengeance is mine; I will repay, saith the Lord."

She chose to serve the devil's purposes, so she would reap the devil's reward. It was time for her to reap the consequences of her actions. Athaliah met her death by the hands of the people that she oppressed. God's children cried out and He answered. He gave them the king that He purposed for them all along. Just trust God. Everyone that seems as if their evil has won, will receive their just due, if they do not repent. They will face the consequences.

Think on These Things

God will position you in places to carry out, train up and present the answer to the prayers of an oppressed and persecuted people. Are you able to look past what you see now, to be a solution for what everyone in the body of Christ will need later? Be patient. God always has a plan and you are a significant part of its execution.

Jehosheba — She Grabbed IT!

Athaliah — She Killed for IT!

5. Jehosheba and Athaliah

Chapter Five Questions

Jehosheba & Athaliah

The Beauty

1. Are you concerned about how the world views you or God's view?

2. God's way are holy and just. But, do you sometimes believe God holds your family's negative dealings against you? If so, why?

3. Are you jealous when others are prospering?

4. Is it difficult to remain faithful to God when the truth is hidden behind closed doors? Write your thoughts down and present your prayers to God concerning this.

5. Are there members of your own family who have done evil things, are dishonest or have mistreated others? How can you pray for them today?

A Prayer for my Sister

Lord, You have allowed my sister to see evil within her family, yet You still have a positive plan for her. Thank You for using her to show that she is responsible for choosing the right way. Thank You for entrusting her as an ambassador of Christ. Help her to hold her peace and await Your perfect timing for restoration. Amen

The Beast

1. On a scale of 1-10 how much do you seek power and position. (10 being very much)

2. Do you believe that God's promises are slack concerning you?

5. Jehosheba and Athaliah

3. What are the characteristics of Jesus?

4. What happens when you go against God's will and make plans for yourself?

A Prayer for My Sister

Father, thank You for your grace and mercy. You have a purpose for my sister. Your plans for her are good and not of evil, to give her an expected end. May she become more compassionate towards Your people and never think of herself more highly than she ought. She shall await Your positioning and ordering of her steps, never harming others to get ahead. Amen

6

<u>Ambitious Achsah</u>

Ask and it shall be given unto you; seek, and ye shall find; knock and it shall be opened unto you. Matthew 7:7-8

"I can make my own decisions. I am independent and can take care of myself. I don't need my husband to act as if he's my father." Whoa! These are comments I hear frequently, when I am conducting premarital counseling with young couples. There is such a desire for singleness, yet the goal is to become husband and wife. After much dialogue and role plays, we expose the factors leading to this thinking. It comes down to control and a lack of submission. Most confuse submission with being subordinate. Neither are less than the other, but God has established how husband and wife have different functions.

Did I mention that I am a licensed and ordained minister? I love serving God's purpose and mentoring young couples is an area I hold dear to my heart. Marriage is sacred, satisfying and serious. During these sessions much is revealed.

I often share specific scriptures with the couples to route them to what the Bible says about marriage like. Ephesians 5:25, "A man ought to love his wife, like Christ loves the church." Or I share the story of Adam and Eve's beginning in Genesis. But the story that seems to really open up the eyes of the wife and address some of her deepest issues, is the one about Caleb's daughter, Achsah. Sometimes we as wives think we have it all figured out.

I lead with this question, "What if you were told who you would marry and had no choice in the matter? How would that make you feel?" Most often the answer is, "I would feel violated. I would like to make my own choices."

There are many things you may take for granted and the freedom of choice could be one of them. In India, Pakistan, Australia and Japan, women don't have a choice in the matter of marriage. Arranged marriages still exist. Much like the story of our next woman of God.

God has given a picture of how He desires us to view what He is doing. Can you pronounce this name? Say it "Achsah." It sounds a bit like "Ask her," so let's do just that.

Her Background

Achsah's story is found in the book of Joshua 15:16. She was Caleb's only daughter. You may be familiar with this faithful man by the name of Caleb because he and Joshua were the only spies out of twelve that believed God at His word about a promised land flowing with milk and honey. She was beautiful and raised in a God-fearing home. It seemed like she had everything, but there was something she could not choose for herself. Something special that God orchestrated to work out on her behalf.

6. Ambitious Achsah

She grew up during a time of arranged marriages. It was the job of her father to choose who was best for his daughter. Who would be the one chosen for her? What would be his occupation? Would he be a military leader, blacksmith or even a tax collector? The details of this great story may have you in suspense. Let's reveal more to see what God teaches us through this amazing story. It was up to the father to matchmake and sadly enough ungodly fathers in days of old would trade their daughters for cattle or sacrifice them to idol gods. How undervalued women were by some men. How would you like to be given away and mistreated with no span of control?

These were the times she faced. But her father had a promise from God that would bless his family for generations to come. It was time for her father to receive his inheritance. A blessing of obedience unto God. Caleb went up to Moses at the ripe old age of 87 to claim his territory. There was only one problem. There were enemies still living on the land. What would her father do in his old age?

The Proposal

Caleb needed someone to conquer his land. He proposed to all of the men, that whoever conquered the land, could have his daughter in marriage. Wait what about Achsah? What if she didn't want to be married? How did her father put her into his plan? Did you catch it? She was a part of her father's plan.

How much better do you feel now knowing you at least have the right to choose. She was what would be referred to as a trophy wife because she became the prize for whoever the winner would be. So now I ask you to ponder this.

Facing IT Forward

Do you believe her father would do something intentionally to hurt her? Remember this was one of God's faithful servants. Truly he would never do anything to hurt his only daughter. It helps when you have a relationship of trust with your father. Like the Lord desires to have with you.

Achsah trusted her father knew best. Do you trust when God is orchestrating things in your life that He is doing it for your good?

Romans 8:28 says, "And we know all things work together for good to those who love God and are the called according to His purpose." God works everything together. He desires to bless you and will not withhold anything from you.

Achsah had to obey and trust that this is what was planned by God. There was one who stepped up to the challenge to conquer the land. What does this mean? This means that one would have to be willing to sacrifice his life for her hand in marriage. Who would do that? His name was Othniel.

How loving is it to know that someone thought you were worth dying for? Sound familiar? Jesus Christ chose to leave His throne and come down to a world that needed saving. God sent Him to die just for you. It was personal and intentional. This was a marriage made in heaven. Jesus was given the church as His bride and even though she didn't understand or know Him, this was arranged by her Father. God always has your best interest at heart. It's all about trusting Him in all things.

What is it that you're facing in your singleness or within your marriage? Are you seeking the Lord for His plans for your life? Did God arrange your marriage? The Bible says in Mark 10:9, "What therefore God has joined together, let not man put asunder." Would this man be successful in winning Achsah?

6. Ambitious Achsah

Othniel defeated the enemy in Caleb's promised land. He has won his bride. Achsah would be given to Othniel, as Caleb promised. It was customary for the father of the bride to bestow land to the newlyweds as a gift. It was for them to have and raise a family and flock. Othniel because of his sacrifice received a wife and land. Sounds like double for his trouble. But here is where God shows you that you have your own identity. What you bring will complement your husband and bless your family.

She Asked for It

As the couple were receiving land, the wisdom of Achsah kicked in. She knew the land her father gave her was lacking what it needed to produce. In order for them to prosper, they needed more and she wasn't afraid to ask for it.

Have you experienced some dry times in your life? Were you productive? Did it seem like something was missing?

Achsah figured it out! She jumped on a donkey and went to her father. (When you have that father – daughter relationship you can do that) She knew what they needed to move forward. She asked him for a spring. Yes, she asked him for water. Achsah knew her family would need water for the cattle, land and for themselves to survive. No water, no life. Her father granted her request and gave her more than what she needed. He gave her the upper spring and the nether springs. Why did she receive? Because she asked for it.

The Bible says in Matthew 7:7, "Ask and ye shall receive, seek and ye shall find, knock and the door shall be opened unto you."

The land was no good without the fresh water source. Water symbolizes life and the Word of God. You are nothing without the Word. It is the only thing that softens the hardened land enough to sow seeds. How often are you watering your land? Don't sacrifice the water. You need it to live.

Achsah was a blessing to her husband. Her timely and bold personality was a compliment to her husband. She was willing to ask for what they needed. But her obedience to her father's will for her life in the beginning is what made her so attractive, a man would risk his life for her hand in marriage. Her husband was willing to take a risk and she was willing to go before her father and ask for what was necessary for their future.

Think on These Things

What are you asking your Father for? How determined are you? Remember we started talking about control, yet we ended with two becoming one by looking out for their future together. They faced it forward! You're a compliment to your husband. God chooses the best for His daughters. What an arrangement.

When you trust God with your future, it is still an arranged marriage! I guess things haven't changed since days of old for marriage.

Ambitious Achsah — She Asked for IT!

Chapter Six Questions

Ambitious Achsah

1. In what areas are your gifts better suited?

2. Do you trust that God has a specific plan for you?

3. How is your relationship with the Lord?

4. What are some of the things you are believing God for?

5. Are there areas in your life that seem to be left wanting? Have you presented those areas to the Lord?

6. Ambitious Achsah

A Prayer for My Sister

Father, thank You for those that have gone before my sister to pave the way. Because of Your Son Jesus Christ, my sister is able to go boldly before Your throne and cast her cares upon You. She has the assurance of knowing that she can ask, seek and knock and You will answer her prayers according to Your will. For You are her Sun and Shield and no good thing will You withhold from those that walk uprightly. I ask these things in the Name of Jesus name. Amen.

7

Dorcas the Disciple

Give and it shall be given to you; good measure, pressed down, and shaken together, and running over, shall men give into your bosom. For with the same measure you use it shall be measured to you again. Luke 6:38

Giving

There are many women who have a heart for giving. What about you? Who is someone in your life that you admire for being a giver and putting others before themselves? I remember watching the Oprah Winfrey show one day and she asked the audience to look up under their seats. There was an envelope under each seat. I was leaning in wondering, what could it be under their seats? The next thing I heard were screams of shock and excitement. Oprah gave every audience member a car. Are you kidding me? Who does that? God through Oprah does. There were audience members who had been praying for a new vehicle. Oprah was in the perfect position to be used to meet their needs. What a day of blessings.

You Are an Answer

You are the answer to the prayers of many as well. Who needs what you have? It's not about money. It's a heart thing. A desire to show your love to others and care enough to help meet a need. What an opportunity you have been given.

Proverbs 19:17 says, "Whoever is generous to the poor lends to the Lord, and He will repay him for his deed."

Are you willing to share your gift with those less fortunate?

In Proverbs 18:16, the Bible says, "Your gift will make room for you and bring you before great men." This doesn't mean that you should give to attract an audience, but because of the God you serve and your heart, people will desire to be in your presence. Like Dorcas, known also as Tabitha in the Bible, an ordinary woman who will show you how giving affects communities.

You can locate her in Acts 9:36-42. This story opens with a description of her. She is described as a disciple. Not that she had long hair, beautiful eyes or had a large tent. She is described as one who adheres to the teachings of another. Dorcas was a follower of Jesus Christ. She was obedient in her worship, as a servant and as a witness. But wait! We need to know more about her. Was she married? Does she have children? Did she have apparent weaknesses?

Do we really need to know more than what God has shared? Needing to get in her business, gives us an opportunity to state opinions and try to figure out her opportunities, just like others are trying to do to you right now.

7. Dorcas the Disciple

Isaiah 54:17 says, "No weapon that is formed against thee shall prosper; every tongue that shall rise against thee in judgement thou shalt condemn. This is the heritage of the servants of the Lord, and their righteousness is of me, saith the Lord."

If God be for you, who can be against you? Weapons will form, but they will not prosper. Keep focused and keep giving.

When Life Turns for the Worse

Dorcas was full of good works and acts of charity. She showed her love through her actions. She seized the opportunity to do good. She was selfless. Character traits you should desire to display.

Then the Bible stuns us and tell us, she became ill and she died. How do you face this forward when life as you know it has ended? What was her illness? What can you learn from a dead woman? Her time has come to an end, but my sister there is more to her. Even in death, she speaks.

Those that loved her, (yes, she was loved) washed her and laid her dead body in the upper room and they weren't family. Sometimes those that care for you intimately aren't your biological family. They are those who are spiritually connected to you. The "care" that she gave others while she was alive was given to her in death. What a picture of devotion.

Community Action

Other disciples were unsettled about this ordinary woman, who was full of good works. She was dead, but they were disturbed about her death. Can't you hear them praying to God to raise her up? I can hear them saying, "Not this one Lord! She is needed and has done so much. We don't want her to die." Heart wrenching! Imagine the prayers that would go up to God from the community who was crying out for this woman to live.

Is there anyone who would fight for you to live? Who have you impacted so much, that they are willing to go before the Lord and scream "Not yet, we need her!"? Sounds like Dorcas lived her purpose. But they didn't stop with how they felt. They put their words in action.

The disciples heard that Apostle Peter was nearby. They had heard about the miracles God did through him. There was an answer nearby and they had to exhaust every opportunity, to find a solution to this problem of death. There is only One who could change this situation. They went urging Peter to come to Joppa. You would think that Peter would have had a lot of questions, since he didn't know them or her. But Peter trusted God. He was an answer lingering in the right place at the right time. The answer is always nearer than you think.

Romans 8:28 says, "All things are working together for good, to those who love God and are the called according to His purpose."

Great things happen when God's people pray. Peter came without delay, to a place that was in need. Their need was great! When Peter arrived the Bible says, the widows were crying, showing him, the things she made while she was with them. Now we get to know a little more about her. She was a seamstress. She made things for those who the Bible tells us to look out for. The widows. She sewed for royalty and used the money she made to clothe widows and those in need. When no one else cared Dorcas did. She used her talent of sewing to make a difference in her community.

Exodus 22:22 says, "You shall not mistreat any widow or fatherless child." Dorcas obeyed what God commanded. A true woman of God. The work that

7. Dorcas the Disciple

she did spoke for her. How's your obedience? What does your work say about you?

Peter proceeded to put the crying and concerned widows out of the upper room to eliminate any distractions. He would need to hear from God on His will in this situation. God is the only One who can resurrect dead things to life. The answer to their prayers is on the way. Will Dorcas live again?

Make Yourself Available for the Miracle

God doesn't always give us what we want, but He gives us what's in His will. Trust that He hears your prayers. Peter didn't make the decision for Dorcas to live, neither can anyone else around you. But he made the decision to go to a place where God's disciple lived and waited for God's instructions. Just to be available makes the difference in the lives of others. Peter moved forward from where he was, to give what he had to someone that he had never met. Can you say the same? No strings attached, looking for nothing in return.

Apostle Peter knelt down and prayed, and turned to her body and said, "Tabitha, (her name in Greek) arise!" A prayer to God for His will and a word spoken over her, caused her body to respond to the Word. Pay attention to what happens next.

Dorcas opened her eyes. When God brings you out of a dead thing, your eyes will be opened. Next when she saw Peter she sat up. Look at her posture. She was back upright. Ready to move forward. How is your posture? Are you ready to rise up?

Who faced a situation for you, when you couldn't help yourself? It's time for you to return the favor. You have the power to be used by God to awaken those that have fallen asleep.

Rise Up

Finally, Peter gave Dorcas his hand. A stranger raised her up. She was given support. Everything she needed to arise, was right in front of her face.

Keep giving and look for nothing in return. There are others sent to you to pray you through things even when you think no one is paying attention.

Dorcas wasn't aware of what was going on in her absence, but I'm sure she was surprised to hear the story of the prayers and the journey that some took, to bring her back to the land of the living. They faced it forward together.

Dorcas lived a life that was bigger than herself and her community felt she was needed. But God used her life and her death to show His glory.

Think on These Things

The miracle of this ordinary woman spread throughout her city and many believed on the Lord. What an impact! Her life and even her death, brought people to Christ. Her giving to God's people was evidence that Jesus loves, lives and saves.

Who recognizes the Lord in you and aren't willing to let you go? He has extraordinary assignments for all of His daughters, according to His purpose.

7. Dorcas the Disciple

She was a woman facing the most dreadful circumstances, but God escorted her to the forefront of our hearts. You are that person for so many others.

Just keep on giving and let the work that you do speak for you. Praise the Lord!

Dorcas the Disciple — She Lived IT!

Chapter Seven Questions

Dorcas the Disciple

1. What is the definition of a disciple?

2. In what ways are you similar to Dorcas?

3. Who benefits from the love you display?

4. Describe your prayer life.

7. Dorcas the Disciple

A Prayer For My Sister

Lord, show my sister how to give away what You have given her. Teach her to see the needs of others and find a way to meet those needs. Allow her guiding light to shine before men so they can see her good words and glorify You. May she live a life that would cause others to seek You. In the name of Jesus, Amen.

8

<u>Conclusion</u>

Thank you for taking the time out to get to know Old and New Testament Women of God to add to your sister circle. These women and their stories testify of impossibilities made possible through those who love and obey God's commandments. Women who faced trying circumstances, yet faced every opportunity moving forward for others to receive a blessing.

As women of God, we must study the examples that God has given us, to have a better understanding of His purpose for His daughters. Sometimes we believe what others say in the negative and allow their words to supersede God's Words. When this negativity penetrates into our inbox, it changes our outlook. This causes us to go back to our old ways of thinking. Moving forward when faced with adversity can be very difficult, but with God all things are possible. We will go through trials and tribulations, but we will make it through them as we face what God has placed before us. My sisters, trust God and keep moving towards your destiny.

Don't believe the mail the enemy sends. Select delete.

God does extraordinary things through ordinary people and women aren't left out, even if no one recognizes your contributions. These women have exposed the actions God desires for us to take. All together they represent growth. It's time for us to mature and prepare to share our trials and triumphs with the next generation of young ladies that are getting ready to rise up.

Think on These Things

Dauntless Daughters of Zelophehad – THEY WAITED FOR IT – Study and get your facts straight. Boldly approach God and make your requests known. Patiently await His answer and watch History change before your very eyes.

Judicious Jael – SHE NAILED IT – When opportunity knocks, let it in and nail it. It will give you peace for times to come.

The Wise Woman of Thebez – SHE DROPPED IT – Let it go and allow God to guide it. You need not hold on to it. It was designed to destroy that which was trying to destroy you.

The Witty Woman of Beth Abel – SHE SPOKE IT – We can learn how to speak up for the existence of community.

Jehosheba – SHE GRABBED IT – Take a chance to grab your future by the hand. Your destiny is at stake, but remember keep things to yourself until God is ready to reveal it.

Athaliah – SHE KILLED FOR IT – Don't appoint yourself to a position. Also don't kill the spirits of others for power's sake. God will elevate you in due time. You don't have to become like the negative influences that you've experienced in your family.

8. Conclusion

Ambitious Achsah – *SHE ASKED FOR IT* – Don't be afraid to ask your father for what you want. Prayer is essential and God hears us when we pray. He does exceeding, abundantly above all we can ask or think.

Dorcas the Disciple – *SHE LIVED IT* – Give and God will give unto you. Meet the needs of others as God shows up for you in your time of need. People will testify of your love.

Now that we have come to the close of this book, be fearlessly ready to face whatever comes your way. Don't become stagnant and don't retreat. FACE IT FORWARD and watch as others are blessed by your testimony.

Action Plan

1. What are three things do you desire to change, as you trust God more?

2. What did these women teach you?

A Prayer for My Sister

Lord, I thank You for my sister. May she realize through these stories You have shared, she is now ready to face whatever challenges You may set before her. May she trust You in all things and encourage another sister to keep moving in Your direction. Bless my sister and her family. In Jesus' name I ask all these things, Amen.

GOD DID IT!

About Nicole

Nicole Jackson is an enthusiastic, energetic corporate trainer, keynote speaker, workshop facilitator, brand ambassador and CEO of Transformers Training, LLC. She delivers powerful and highly motivational keynote messages and provides one-on-one coaching and workshops on the subjects of leadership, team building, customer service and youth initiatives. Clients include Cactus Flower, Rare Gems Transitions Inc., Picture Me Perfect 3D/4D imaging, Whataburger, The Jon Gordon Company and more. For more than twenty years, she has worked as a leader in the Quick Services Restaurant industry, providing staff and leadership training.

Nicole is the recipient of numerous awards, including The Faces of Diversity Award from the National Restaurant Association, The Americans With Disabilities Award, and The Make A Difference Award. She was awarded the key to the city of Milton, Florida, for servant leadership. A certified Jon Gordon Companies Trainer, Nicole has earned her Masters Degree in Theology from International Miracle Institute and is currently studying for a Bachelor's Degree in Communication from Regent University. Nicole attended West Florida Baptist Institute of Pensacola, FL, where she has certifications in Bible Analysis and Defense of the Faith. Nicole received her doctoral degree in Christian Theology. She has several certifications in Training and Development. Nicole has been leading and developing teams throughout the Florida Panhandle for over two decades. An ordained minister, Nicole is a favored speaker at conferences and revivals throughout Florida and the Southeast. She enjoys singing and writing her own songs.

She is a wife to Antonio Jackson, mother to Alex, Cierrah and Ashelynn and grandmother of three. Nicole enjoys Bible study, fishing, baking and a good cup of coffee. Her family makes their home in Milton, FL.

Nicole Jackson's Contact Information

Nicole Myers Jackson

P.O. Box 4619

Milton, Fl 32572

www.nicolejacksongroup.com

njackson1972@yahoo.com

(850)313-0989

Made in the USA
Middletown, DE
27 August 2019